Kingfisher Books, Grisewood & Dempsey Ltd,
Elsley House, 24-30 Great Titchfield Street,
London W1P 7AD

First published in 1993 by Kingfisher Books
2 4 6 8 10 9 7 5 3 1

Material in this edition was previously published by
Kingfisher Books in *Animal Life Stories*: *The Tiger* in
1988 and in *Wildlife Library*: *The Tiger* in 1978.

British Library Cataloguing in Publication Data
A catalogue record for this book is available from
the British Library
ISBN 1 85697 085 X

Series editor: Veronica Pennycook
Series designer: Terry Woodley
Cover illustration by Doreen McGuinness/Garden Studio
Illustration on pp 6-7 by John Butler
Typeset in 3B2
Phototypeset by SPAN
Printed in Great Britain by
BPCC Paulton Books Limited

The Tiger

Angela Royston

Illustrated by Graham Allen

Kingfisher Books

In this book

The tiger in this story is an Indian tiger. It lives in forests and grasslands. Other kinds of wild tiger live throughout Asia.

The tiger is the largest member of the cat family. Its striped coat helps it to hide among the forest shadows when it is hunting. Tigers are excellent hunters and they kill mainly deer, wild pigs and antelope.

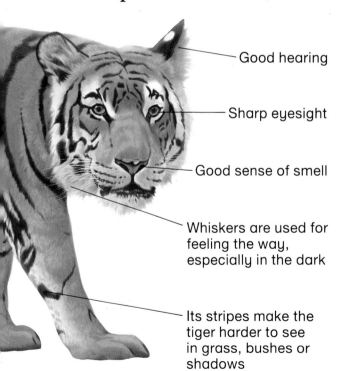

Good hearing

Sharp eyesight

Good sense of smell

Whiskers are used for feeling the way, especially in the dark

Its stripes make the tiger harder to see in grass, bushes or shadows

Dawn in the forest

A female tiger is moving quietly through the forest. She sees some deer and quickly sinks down into the tall grass.

Suddenly one of the deer senses danger and darts away. The other deer follow him.

A short rest

The tiger is not hungry so she doesn't give chase. This time the deer have escaped.

Coming across a clearing, the tiger settles down to wash. She licks herself with her rough tongue.

A loud roar coming from some nearby trees makes the tiger prick up her ears.

A second tiger

She roars back and another tiger appears from the bushes. The second tiger is a male.

At first he is careful not to get too close in case she attacks him. But the tigress lets him stay with her. Soon they mate.

For some days the tigers stay
together, hunting and resting, and
wading in the river to keep cool.

One morning another male tiger
appears through the trees. The
tigress lies there watching him, but
her mate roars loudly to tell him to
keep away.

The cave

One day the tiger pads off into the forest. The tigress will not see him again.

When it is nearly time for her cubs to be born, she sets off to search for a safe place. She walks and walks, until at last she finds a dry cave hidden among a pile of rocks.

For the next few days the tigress stays close to the cave. She hunts a lot now because when her cubs arrive she will not be able to leave them to find food.

One night three small cubs are born. Their eyes are tightly shut. For several days they do nothing but feed and sleep.

The missing cub

After two weeks the cubs open their eyes and begin exploring their cave home.

Their mother has been feeding them on her milk and she is now hungry and thin. She leaves the cave to hunt, not noticing some wild dogs prowling nearby.

One of the dogs sneaks into the cave. Two cubs are asleep and well hidden, but the third is nosing round the entrance, trying to find the way out.

The dog seizes the tiny cub and carries it away. When the tigress comes back from her hunt she finds only two cubs.

Moving the cubs

The tiger does not rest but moves the cubs immediately. She picks one up by the scruff of the neck and carries him to a patch of tall, thick grass. Then she goes back for the second cub.

In this safe hiding place the cubs
grow bigger and stronger every
day. They spend a lot of time
sleeping, or playing happily while
their mother watches. They have
play fights with each other which
test their growing strength.

Playing together

One of the cubs' best games is
pouncing on their mother's
long, swishing tail.

Sometimes they stalk each other through the grass. One cub slowly creeps up and then suddenly pounces on the other. These stalking games help them learn how to hunt their prey.

Wounded

The tigress and her cubs are playing one day, when they see a huge buffalo. The cubs watch as the tigress stalks, and then pounces.

But the buffalo is too strong for her. Its sharp horns knock the tigress to the ground. Luckily she is not badly hurt.

As the months go by, the cubs slowly learn to be good hunters. Sometimes the tigress knocks an animal down and stands back to let the cubs finish the kill.

Hunting alone

One night when the cubs are a year old the bigger cub goes off to hunt alone. While he is crouching quietly by a river, a family of wild pigs comes to drink. The young tiger watches and waits.

All of a sudden he springs and makes his first kill. He drags the pig to some bushes to hide it from other animals. Then he goes to fetch his mother and sister so they can share his meal.

Growing up

As another year passes, the cubs grow into big, sleek tigers. They hunt on their own more and more.

By the time that they are two years old, they can look after themselves and are ready to leave their mother.

The tigress will soon mate again and she'll have a new litter of cubs to look after in the forest.

Some special words

Buffalo A large animal like an ox.

Cub A baby or young tiger.

Litter A group of cubs born together. Tigers usually give birth to two or three cubs at a time.

Prey An animal that is hunted and killed for food by another animal.

Stalking The tiger stalks its prey by creeping slowly and silently towards the animal until it is near enough to pounce.

Tigress A female tiger. She is slightly smaller than male tigers.

Index